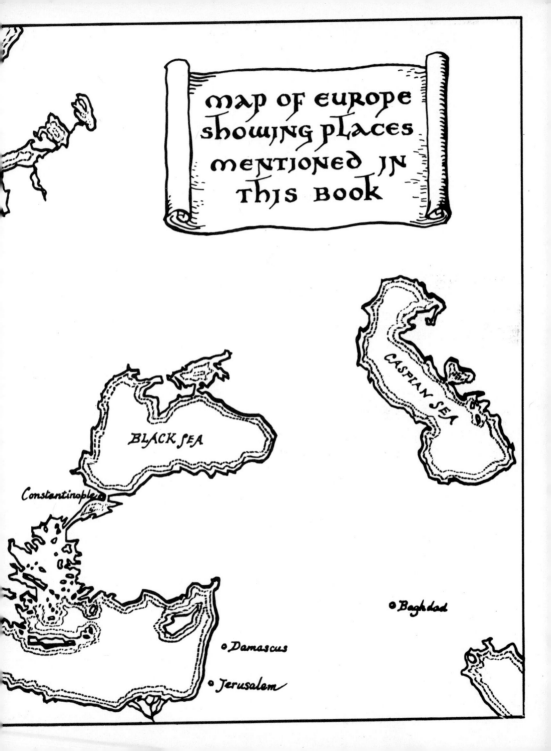

MADE IN THE MIDDLE AGES

ALEXANDER THE GREAT
*from the Nine Heroes
Tapestries
French, 14th century*

Made in the Middle Ages

Written and illustrated by
Christine Price

E. P. DUTTON & COMPANY, INC., NEW YORK

FOR MY MOTHER

who first showed me the glories of the Middle Ages

FOREWORD

THE MEDIEVAL OBJECTS IN THIS BOOK COME FROM museums and libraries in England and the United States. I am very grateful to the Bodleian Library, Oxford; the British Museum; the Metropolitan Museum of Art; the Pierpont Morgan Library; the Victoria and Albert Museum; and the Yale University Art Gallery for their courtesy in giving me permission to include items from their collections.

I would also like to thank Miss Elizabeth Chase, of the Yale University Art Gallery, for reading the manuscript of the book and for making many helpful suggestions.

The list of sources at the end of the book shows which objects belong to each museum or library. I hope it may also serve as a guide to anyone interested in seeing for himself these and many other exciting things that were made in the Middle Ages.

C. P.

CONTENTS

Part II *Things Made for the Church*

MADE IN THE MIDDLE AGES

The Craftsmen and Their World

OST PEOPLE, WHEN THEY THINK OF THE Middle Ages, think of castles and knights in armor or of great cathedrals, built for the worship of God. They call that distant time the Age of Knighthood and Chivalry or the Age of Faith. Yet a bird's-eye view of Europe six hundred years ago, in the fourteenth century, would show us far more than castles and churches.

Around the walls of the castles we would see clustered villages where the knights' tenants lived, farming the land, tending sheep and cattle and pasturing hogs in the forest. We would see the towers of the churches rising above walled towns with market squares and narrow twisting streets of little shops; and along the coasts there would be busy seaports

Above,
PLOWMAN AND HIS TEAM
from the Luttrell Psalter
English manuscript,
14th century

10

with ships unloading cargoes of silks and velvets from Italy, wine from France, Russian furs and English broadcloth, ivory from Africa and costly spices from the East.

On the roads between the towns we would see merchants with strings of loaded pack horses, and here and there the glint of sunlight on steel as a company of men-at-arms rode by, the retainers of some great lord. We might even watch an army besieging a castle in one of the many private wars between rival barons, and looking across the countryside of France, we would see burned villages, trampled fields and people left homeless by the Hundred Years' War between France and England.

The men and women of the Middle Ages lived in a violent, dangerous world, but they were not gloomy folk. They loved bright color and rich decoration. Knights went to war in suits of armor that were

11

AQUAEMANALES, OR WATER JUGS

masterpieces of art; priests wore splendid vestments, embroidered with gold and gems; houses were gaily painted and churches blazed with color, inside and out. All this, and much more, was the work of the medieval craftsmen.

There were no factories in those days for making clothes and furniture and the hundred-and-one things needed for daily living. The tailors and carpenters, weavers and potters did their work by hand, slowly and carefully, and the craftsmen believed that everything, even a useful thing like a water jug, should be good to look at.

ARMORER AT WORK

12

Much of what they made has been lost. Such
fragile luxuries as silk gowns and jewelry are easily
destroyed, and common everyday tools like pots and
pans, spades and plowshares, are worn out and
thrown away. The things that have lasted through
the centuries have often been preserved by accident,
hidden away in odd corners of churches and castles.
You can see some of these treasures today in museums. Each object is labeled with the date, or at
least the century, when it was made, and usually with
the place of its making as well. But what about the
man who made it? Who were these craftsmen?

We seldom know their names. Very rarely did they
sign their work. At the Cloisters in New York you
can see a beautiful silver chalice made in the thirteenth century; engraved around its base is a Latin
inscription which reads: "In honor of the Blessed

13

THE BERTINUS CHALICE

Virgin Mary Brother Bertinus made me in the year of Our Lord 1222."

Like many other craftsmen of the Middle Ages, Brother Bertinus was a monk and lived in a monastery, devoting himself to work, prayer and study. The monasteries were islands of peace in that warlike world, and they grew very wealthy, farming wide tracts of land and receiving lavish gifts from kings and nobles. Monks were particularly skilled in making books, vestments and altar vessels for the Church, like Brother Bertinus' chalice. They worked with gold, silver and precious stones and made tiny delicate carvings in ivory.

The monasteries were centers of fine craftsmanship throughout the Middle Ages, but every town also had its craftsmen. They sold their work in small shops, usually in their own houses, and men of the same craft lived along the same street—shoemakers in one street, goldsmiths in another, armorers here, painters there.

By the fourteenth and fifteenth centuries most of the crafts were organized into guilds. The master craftsmen, heads of the guilds, were wealthy and respected citizens of their towns. In medieval London they used to lead the guildsmen in procession through the streets on special occasions, perhaps to welcome a new Lord Mayor of the city or to celebrate

MEDIEVAL SHOP

14

the King's return from battle. Then the streets were decorated with tapestries and painted banners, people crowded to watch the procession and the craftsmen rode proudly, each man dressed in the brightly colored livery or uniform of his guild.

But the main aim of the craft guilds was to keep up a high standard of workmanship. Working hours were fixed, lasting from dawn to dusk, and the guilds made strict rules for the training of their members.

A boy who wanted to be a painter, for instance, was bound as an apprentice to a master painter for two or three years, or even as long as seven. When he had learned the essentials of his craft, he was employed by the master as a journeyman, a man who worked by the day. Many men were journeymen all their lives. To become a master the young painter had to paint a "masterpiece," an example of his finest work, and submit it to the heads of the painters' guild. They then decided whether he was worthy to be a master and to set up his own shop with journeymen and apprentices under him.

PAINTER AT WORK

With such a thorough training it is no wonder that the guildsmen knew their craft, or "mystery" as they called it. Today, when their work is shown in museums, it often looks as fresh and lovely as on the day it was finished, hundreds of years ago.

The Middle Ages lasted for centuries and it is

hard to say when they began or ended. In this book we shall look only at those things made between the year 1000, when the Vikings discovered America, and the year 1500, just after Columbus had proved that the world was round.

What a bewildering variety there is! Some things are large and impressive, others small enough to slip into your pocket. How were they all made and why? What was the use of this queer-shaped piece of metalwork, this splendid embroidery or that carved ivory statuette? Can they tell us anything about the kind of people who used them, the people of the Middle Ages?

PART I
Things made for the castle

JOUSTING ARMOR
German, about 1500

aRmoR aNd weapoNs

LL THROUGH THE MIDDLE AGES KNIGHTS rode to battle in armor. Wars were so frequent that the armorers were kept busy making new suits of armor and repairing old ones. They had to work to the highest standards, for in battle the lives of kings and great leaders depended on the excellence of their armor.

As weapons and methods of fighting changed, armor had to change to keep pace with them. In 1066, when William the Conqueror and his Norman knights invaded England, they wore simple conical helmets and light shirts of mail or of overlapping metal scales. At the end of the fifteenth century a knight taking part in a tournament was protected by heavy steel plates.

19

NORMAN KNIGHT
11th century

SHIRT OF MAIL
German, 14th century

Mail was made of many small links. If you look
at the fineness of the mesh, you will understand why
making it by hand required a high degree of craftsmanship. It might take months to make a complete
suit of mail. Each link had to be forged separately.
The armorer heated and hammered out a small
iron bar on his anvil until it was long and thin.
Then he wound it around a slender rod to form a coil
of little rings, cut off one ring after another and
linked them together, fastening each ring with a
rivet. Padded coats and caps were worn underneath
the mail and these were made by a "linen armorer."

The Crusaders who fought in the Holy Land
were clad in mail from head to foot. Over it they
wore a long loose surcoat of linen or silk which
helped to protect them from the fierce heat of the
sun. By the thirteenth century the small conical

POMMEL FROM
A SWORD HILT
French, 1245

20

helmet had been replaced by a large iron helm, covering the knight's head and face; and it became the custom for each man to have his own special device painted or embroidered on his surcoat, to show who he was. This device, known as a coat of arms, also appeared on his shield and on the harness and long flowing "trapper" of his horse.

A royal or knightly family was proud of its coat of arms which no one else had the right to wear. The choice of colors and designs was governed by the rules of heraldry. Some coats of arms were simple geometrical patterns; others were devices of trees, birds, animals or fish, and a knight with a lion on his shield often had a crest, in the shape of a lion, mounted on the top of his helm. The tiny shield opposite bears the arms of a French Crusader and once decorated the hilt of his sword.

21

HARNESS DECORATIONS
Spanish, 14th century

This basinet, the commonest kind of helmet in the late fourteenth century, is fitted with a movable visor and is a splendid example of the armorer's craft. To make a basinet the armorer took a plate of steel and slowly worked it into shape by hammering it over a "stake," a small, specially formed anvil set into a block of wood. He did not heat the metal to make it easier to work; hammering the cold steel produced a helmet that was harder and more resistant to blows. The suit of armor on the left includes a basinet and a combination of mail and plate armor. The body protection is a steel brigandine covered with cloth. At the right is a suit made of smooth steel plates, showing the wonderful fifteenth-century armor.

The great armorers of this time signed their work with their marks. The craftsmen of Augsburg in Germany rivaled those of northern Italy where the armorer's skill was passed down from father to son in the Missaglia family of Milan. In the big workshops each craftsman probably specialized in making one part of the complete armor, or "harness" as it was often called. A differently shaped stake was used for hammering out each piece—the breastplate, the shoulder pieces or pauldrons, the gauntlets for the hands and greaves for the legs.

SUIT OF ARMOR
Italian, about 1400

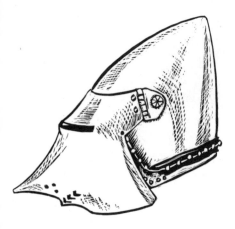

BASINET WITH VISOR
Italian, 1380

BASINET WORN
WITHOUT VISOR

GOTHIC ARMOR
Italian, 1460

ARMORER
MAKING A HELMET

KNIGHT'S SPUR
French, about 1400

DAGGER
North French,
15th century

Spurs were a necessary part of the equipment of knights and men-at-arms on horseback. Only a knight had the right to wear golden spurs, and he could "win his spurs" only after many years of training.

Like the craftsman who worked first as an apprentice, the knight began his training as a page, at the age of nine or ten. In the castle of a lord or at a king's palace he learned to be well-mannered and courteous, to ride a horse and to handle knightly weapons—sword, lance and dagger.

The quintain was used for practice with the lance. This boy holds his lance "couched" under his right arm, just as he will do when he is a mounted knight charging at the enemy. If he does not strike the shield squarely in the middle when he runs at the

QUINTAIN
from the Romance of Alexander
French manuscript, 14th century

quintain, the wooden arm will swing around and the bag will hit him in the back.

In his early teens the boy became a squire. A knight might have several squires to follow him into battle, to carry his shield and to take charge of his horses. If a squire distinguished himself in war he was knighted on the battlefield by the accolade, a light blow on the shoulder with a sword. Otherwise the ceremony of his knighthood was long and elaborate. It included a whole night of prayer and meditation in a church and ended in the morning with the accolade and the fastening on of the new golden spurs. A knight had to be truthful, fight for the right and defend the weak; and throughout his life his sword was his constant companion.

In the old medieval stories knightly swords were often given names. King Arthur's sword, Excalibur, was an enchanted weapon which came to him by magic. The sword of the Emperor Charlemagne, with which he fought the Saracens in Spain in the eighth century, was called Joyeuse (Joyful), and his gallant nephew Roland had a sword named Durendal. *The Song of Roland* tells us that when Roland lay dying, after the Battle of Roncesvalles, he tried

PAINTED SHIELD
German, 15th century

to break his sword rather than let it fall into the hands of the Saracens. He struck it on a rock with all his might, but the good blade would not break.

Some of the best swords were made in Spain by the swordsmiths of Toledo and Valencia. German swords from Cologne were also famous, and the blades of Milan could cut through iron.

Besides their swords and lances, knights used war hammers and maces, evil-looking metal clubs. Daggers were worn by everyone as an ordinary part of dress, and their handles were often delicately carved.

Some of the knight's followers in battle were foot soldiers carrying halberds; others were crossbowmen and archers armed with the longbow, the weapon of Robin Hood. English archers were well-known and

IVORY DAGGER HILT
Venetian, about 1300

26

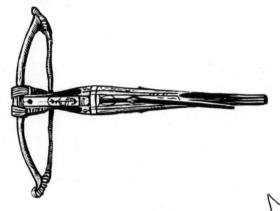

CROSSBOW
Hungarian, 1489

respected in the fourteenth century; their arrows had routed an army of French knights at the Battle of Crécy in 1346. The English also used small cannon at this battle, but these early guns were not powerful or dependable enough to do much damage.

Plate armor was supposed to be proof against all weapons, and before a finished suit left the armorer's shop it was "proved" by being struck at close range with an iron bolt from a crossbow. The plates were beautifully shaped to deflect blows and jointed to let the wearer move with ease. An active man was not helpless in his armor if he were unhorsed. Really cumbersome armor was worn only for show and for tournaments when speed of movement was not necessary.

Tournaments were the great sport of knights. In the early days they were rough battles in which men were killed, and jousts between single knights were often fought to the death. But by the late Middle

27

HALBERDS
Swiss, 15th century

KNIGHTS TILTING

Ages tournaments were hedged around with rules, and the knight and his horse were so amply protected that fatal accidents were rare.

Jousting knights were even prevented from colliding with each other by a barrier called a tilt, and the sport was then known as tilting. The points of the lances were blunted and each competitor tried to strike his opponent hard enough to unhorse him or to break a lance against his helm or his breastplate.

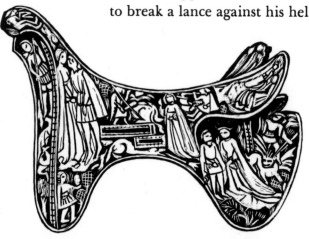

DECORATED SADDLE
German, 1400

28

Contestants were announced by heralds with a fanfare of trumpets. Heraldry was most important at a tournament, and the heavily armored knights were known by their coats of arms.

A tournament was an occasion for wonderful pageantry and display. This elegant saddle, made of wood covered with engraved staghorn, gives us some idea of the bewildering richness of decoration we might see around the tiltyard. Knights vied with each other in the magnificence of their armor, their painted shields and banners and the trappings of their horses. Their ladies gave them favors to carry into battle, perhaps a veil to drape from the helm or a necklace to wear; and all the spectators—men, women and children—were dressed in their gayest clothes, the ordinary folk in woolen cloth of red and blue, the nobility in glowing silks and velvets.

WATCHING A TOURNAMENT
Detail from a painting on a marriage chest, Italian, 15th century

PRINTED LINEN
*German, 13th or
14th century*

cloth and clothing

LOTHES DO NOT LAST AS WELL AS AR-
mor. Linens, woolens and silks worn
in the Middle Ages have come down
to us mostly as fragments, and we
have to look at medieval pictures
and statues to see how the people dressed and how
fashions changed.

Wool and linen had been spun and woven in
Europe from earliest times. Linen was made into
underwear, shirts, babies' clothes and women's head-
dresses. Wool was the material for outer clothes—
cloaks, gowns, tunics and the long hose worn by
the men—and large quantities of woolen cloth were
made in the Middle Ages.

Many people did their own spinning and weaving

30

WOMAN SPINNING WITH
A DISTAFF

at home, using the wool from their own sheep, but in towns and villages cloth was produced by guilds of professional craftsmen. The Flemish cities of Bruges, Ypres, Ghent and Brussels were well-known for their fine woolens. The great sheep farms of England supplied abundant wool for the Flemish weavers and also for the making of English cloth. By the fifteenth century English broadcloths were sold throughout Europe and as far away as Africa and the Near East.

Many different craftsmen took part in producing these woolen fabrics. They often worked at home, directed by a rich merchant who bought the raw wool and sold the finished cloth.

The wool was first carded or combed and then spun, usually by women who were known as "spinsters." The weavers, or "websters," wove narrow cloth on a single loom; broadcloth, two yards wide, needed a

LINEN FIBERS CAME
FROM FLAX PLANTS.

SHEARING SHEEP

WEAVING ON
A SINGLE LOOM

double loom at which two weavers sat side by side.

The lengths of woven cloth went to the fuller who trampled on them in a trough of water until the threads were matted together. The wet cloth was stretched on a frame called a tenter and then brushed with the prickly heads of the teasel plant to pull up the loose fibers. These were trimmed off by a shearer and the fabric smoothly finished.

SHEARING CLOTH

The dyers might dye the wool, the spun yarn or the finished cloth. The most usual dye was blue, made from the dried leaves of the woad plant. Red came from madder roots and saffron yellow from the stamens of the autumn crocus.

Woolen materials, coarse or fine, were worn by everyone; but more and more, wealthy people demanded the luxury of silk. Since the days of Charlemagne silk had been imported into Europe from China, India and Japan. Camel caravans carried the silk on the dangerous journey across Asia to Constantinople; then the precious cargo went by ship to Greece and up the Adriatic Sea to Venice.

DYEING CLOTH

A legend says that silkworms and the secrets of rearing them were smuggled out of China in the sixth century and brought to Constantinople by two Greek monks. Silkworms probably came to Sicily and Spain with the invading Saracens three centuries later. The Saracens were fine silk weavers and produced in Spain a material called sarcenet which was greatly favored in medieval England. Heavy silk called baldachin came from Bagdad, and damask from Damascus. Other favorite materials were samite, ciclatoun, sendal and taffeta, names in which we seem to hear the rustle of the silk.

In the twelfth and thirteenth centuries the cities of Italy—Venice, Lucca and Florence—were centers of silk weaving, and the craft spread to France, Germany and England. This German silk has an animal design printed on it with wood blocks to imitate the more costly Italian fabrics which had woven patterns. The design was probably copied from a Near Eastern silk.

13TH-CENTURY
COSTUMES

PRINTED SILK
German, 13th or 14th century

Opposite, SILK BROCADE
Italian, 14th century

After the Venetian traveler, Marco Polo, returned from his years in China at the court of Kublai Khan, Chinese patterns became popular in Italy. The flying phoenix birds on this fragment of Italian satin are a Chinese idea. Threads of silver and gold were often added to these silken materials to make rich brocades. The fabric design on the opposite page was originally woven in purple thread wound around with the thinnest gold wire, but through the years the gold has worn away. The same kind of thread was used in weaving cloth of gold for royal robes.

Velvet, first made in Europe in the thirteenth century, was woven in such a way that little loops of thread stood up all over the surface of the fabric. To make "cut velvet" the loops were cut by hand, giving the stuff a soft, luxurious pile. In the fifteenth century, the Italian cities produced splendid velvets with large bold patterns.

BROCADED SATIN
Italian, 14th century

34

5TH-CENTURY
OSTUMES

VELVET
Italian,
15th century

By the late Middle Ages the old simplicity in dress had gone, and the clothes of knights and ladies were as varied and brilliant as a flower garden. When the patterns were not woven or printed onto the material, they were worked in embroidery. The coats of arms of knights were embroidered on the robes of their ladies. People blossomed out in gowns and doublets patterned with trees, birds and animals, even letters of the alphabet and notes of music.

Embroideries in threads of silk, gold and silver were made richer still by the addition of jewels—rubies, sapphires and pearls. Such clothes were ruinously expensive, and a nobleman might wear half his fortune on his back. Jewelry was an important item for the well-dressed person. Medieval people loved the sparkle of gems, but they valued jewelry for other reasons too, as we shall see.

Left and opposite,
15TH-CENTURY COSTUMES

jewels and enamels

EWELRY WAS LARGELY MADE BY GOLD-smiths. They were among the most skilled craftsmen of the Middle Ages, for theirs was the delicate work of smelting precious metals, making enamel inlay and cutting and mounting gems. They kept their supplies of gold and jewels in strong chests and sometimes they stored other men's valuables for safekeeping. As a result, some goldsmiths became rich bankers and moneylenders. In England the goldsmiths' guild was founded in 1180, and a few years later one of the guildsmen became Lord Mayor of London.

The goldsmiths of Florence had their shops on the Ponte Vecchio, the old bridge over the Arno, and

GOLD BROOCHES

GOLD RING
Venetian,
13th century

37

SILVER SIGNET RINGS
15th century

those of Paris lived along two bridges across the Seine. Their shops were small and cramped. A counter faced the street and in the workroom behind sat the master and his apprentices, making brooches and gold chains, pendants and finger rings.

Rings were always popular, whatever the fashion in clothes, and were worn on the thumb as well as on all four fingers.

These two signet rings combine beauty with usefulness. A signet ring was engraved with the initials of its owner, or if he were a merchant, with the same "merchant's mark" that was painted on his packages of goods. When he wrote a letter or signed a document, he put his seal on it by pressing the signet ring onto a spot of melted wax and leaving his mark there.

Rings set with precious stones were supposed to have strong magic powers. This gold ring set with a sapphire was expected to cure eye diseases and protect its owner against poisoning. An opal, when wrapped in a bay leaf, was supposed to make a man invisible. An agate stone made him amiable and an eloquent speaker, and a jacinth would put him to sleep. This ring, set with a wolf's tooth instead of a jewel, has a secret charm engraved inside it which

GOLD RING WITH
SAPPHIRE
14th century

GOLD RING WITH
WOLF'S TOOTH

would not only cure toothache but also calm storms and tempests!

Religious mottoes were often inscribed on rings, and this "decade ring" could even be used as a rosary for private prayer, the eleven knobs around it standing for eleven beads on the rosary. The picture of Saint Christopher engraved on the ring must have made it doubly valuable to its owner, for one look at Saint Christopher, the patron saint of travelers, would keep a man safe from harm for a whole day.

Love rings, shaped like clasped hands, were inscribed with suitable verses. They were called "posy rings," from the French word *poésie* (poetry), and as a knight commonly gave flowers to his lady along with the rings, a bunch of flowers came to be called a posy.

Brooches made elegant presents too, and this gold heart-shaped brooch has on it the words in Old French VOUS ESTES MA IOY MONDEINE ("You are my earthly joy").

Round brooches and decorated belt buckles were worn in the early Middle Ages, but the dress of those days was too plain to allow for much jewelry. With the coming of richer dress materials styles changed,

GOLD DECADE RING
English, 15th century

SILVER-GILT RING
English, 15th century

ENAMELED PENDANT
French, 14th century

HEART-SHAPED BROOCH
14th century

39

as we have seen. Jewelry became more elaborate, and women's low-necked gowns brought necklaces and pendants into fashion. The pendant on page 39 was made in the French town of Limoges, famous for enamels done by the champlevé method.

To do this work the craftsman drew his design on a copper plate and then chiseled away little hollows in the metal to hold the enamel inlay. He applied the inlay in the form of a paste made from powdered glass of different colors—red, white, green and rich shades of blue. Then he heated the work until the enamel fused together and united with the copper, and when it was cool the craftsman smoothed and polished it. He gilded the exposed parts of the copper, often decorating them first with engraving.

The delicate designs of the Byzantine necklace are done in a different kind of enamel work, called cloisonné. Here the pattern has been drawn on gold instead of copper, and colored paste laid in tiny enclosures, known as *cloisons*, between raised lines of thin gold wire.

The narrow belt from a woman's gown is plated with silver gilt and little enamels. There were no

pockets in medieval clothes, and women's belts were loaded down with purses, household keys, small knives, scissors and round mirrors of metal or glass in ivory cases.

The little ivory box below, which might have been used to hold a lady's jewels, is carved with scenes from the tragic story of Tristram and Isolde, one of the long series of tales about King Arthur and his knights of the Round Table. These and other medieval romances were well-known. Most people did not read them in books but heard them told by minstrels who wandered from place to place, telling stories and singing songs in castles, towns and villages. Almost everyone enjoyed a good story, and listening to the minstrels' tales was one of the favorite pastimes of the Middle Ages.

KEYS
14th century

THE TRISTRAM CASKET
Rhenish, about 1200

41

TRUMPETS AND CYMBALS

Sports and Pastimes

MEDIEVAL PEOPLE LOVED MUSIC. MUSI-cians appear again and again in paintings, sculptures and tapestries and in the books of the Middle Ages. The pictures on these two pages are taken from two great Psalters, or Books of Psalms, and from a copy of the *Romance of Alexander*, one of the most famous minstrels' tales. All three books are decorated with many small drawings which often have nothing to do with the text. Instead, they show the daily life of the fourteenth century, when the books were made, and give us a vivid idea of how people amused themselves.

Minstrels played harps and fiddles and many kinds of wind instruments, from bagpipes to organs; and

PLAYING A MANDORA

42

BAGPIPES

DANCE AND SONG

wandering jugglers did their tricks. There were
amateur musicians and singers too, and groups of
people enjoyed a dance in the castle hall.

Through the long winter evenings they played in-
door games, including boisterous ones such as blind-
man's buff, but the favorite game was chess.

Like silks and spices, chess came to Europe from
the East. The Italians played it as early as the
eleventh century; the Viking seafarers probably

JUGGLER

PUPPET SHOW
Right, A GAME OF
BOB-APPLE

PLAYING CHESS OUTDOORS

IVORY CHESSMAN
North European
12th or 13th century

learned it in Constantinople when they sailed up the Mediterranean in their dragon-headed long ships. The Vikings prided themselves on their skill at chess and carried the game to remote parts of Europe. This ivory knight from a chess set was found on an island in the Hebrides, off the coast of Scotland. Mounted on his stocky northern pony, he is dressed like the twelfth-century warriors who moved him on the chessboard. They played for high stakes, and it was not unknown for an irate player to hit his opponent on the head with the board and knock him flat.

Backgammon, also called "tables," was played on a board with dice and round pieces and was almost as popular among the nobility as chess. This ivory

IVORY CHESSMAN
English or
Scandinavian,
12th century

44

piece is carved in an exciting design of Samson slaying the Philistines, perhaps to inspire the player to
press on to victory!

Out-of-doors the best-loved sports were falconry
and hunting. This carved case from a lady's small
mirror shows a couple out hawking. They carry the
trained falcons on their left hands which are protected by heavy gloves. When game is sighted, the
falcons will be let loose to soar high in the sky and
swoop down on wild duck, partridge or heron.

A GAME OF
BLIND-MAN'S BUFF

**LADY WITH
A FALCON**
Early 15th century

TapeSTRIES

SCENES OF HAWKING AND HUNTING APpear in tapestries too. This small tapestry was made in the fifteenth century, perhaps as a gift for a noble lady like the one in the design. It was probably woven at Arras, a town which in its heyday belonged to Flanders and was so famous for fine weaving that the word "arras" became another name for tapestry.

The designer of a medieval tapestry did not do the weaving himself. His large drawing, made on a piece of linen, was hung up as a guide to the weaver, and the main lines of the design were also drawn on the strong warp threads stretched between rollers on the

LOW-WARP LOOM WITH TREADLES ATTACHED TO THE WARP THREADS TO MAKE THE WORK QUICKER

HIGH-WARP LOOM

47

Above, DANDELION *from The Lady with a Falcon*

loom. These threads were vertical on the high-warp loom and horizontal on the low-warp. The tapestry weaver worked on the wrong side of his material and used threads of linen, silk or wool which were thick enough to cover the warp completely. Each of his fifteen or twenty colors was wound on a separate bobbin. He picked up the bobbins, one after another, as he needed them, weaving an inch or two of blue to make a flower or a tiny strip of green for a leaf. The colors have lasted well, and even in the oldest tapestries we can still see something of the rich reds and blues that delighted the people of the Middle Ages.

Tapestries were used as wall hangings and curtains, and helped to keep out drafts in the cold rooms of medieval castles. Even a poor knight liked to have a few gay tapestries to cover the gray walls of his hall, and a wealthy man might own hundreds of them. When kings and nobles moved from one castle to another, as they often did, they carried along wagonloads of tapestries, and in wartime favorite hangings might decorate a nobleman's tent on the battlefield.

Many yards of tapestries were needed to cover a single room, and they were often made in sets. Among the oldest surviving tapestries is a set of three, known as The Nine Heroes, woven in 1385

KNIGHT AND TWO LADIES
from the tapestry of
The Hebrew Heroes

for the Duke of Berry, a great nobleman of France.

Each tapestry pictures three heroes of history and legend. There are three pagan heroes—Hector, Alexander and Julius Caesar; three Hebrews—David, Joshua and Judas Maccabaeus; and three Christians —King Arthur, Charlemagne and Godfrey de Bouillon. The names of these heroes were well-known when the tapestries were made; Alexander, King Arthur and Charlemagne were especially famous because of the tales told about them by minstrels. Godfrey de Bouillon was the most recent of the heroes, a gallant French knight who was a leader in the First Crusade to the Holy Land.

Although nearly all these men lived in ancient times, the designer of the tapestries has dressed them in armor of his own period and surrounded them with little figures that he might easily have drawn from life. They are just the sort of people the artist would have seen at the Duke's palace at Bourges where the tapestries were made—knights and men-at-arms and archers, ladies with their pets and minstrels playing a tambourine and a viol.

JULIUS CAESAR AND TWO
MINSTRELS
*from the tapestry of
The Pagan Heroes*

49

THE UNICORN AT THE FOUNTAIN
Late 15th century

Another beautiful set of tapestries illustrates the strange story of a unicorn hunt. Five of these seven tapestries were woven at the end of the fifteenth century, the other two a little later. The first five were probably made as a present for Anne of Brittany when she was married to King Louis XII of France in 1499. Anne's monogram—AE—often appears in the design of the pictures, and if you look carefully you will find it five times in The Unicorn at the Fountain.

In this tapestry, the second of the series, you see the hunters and their hounds closing around the unicorn while he dips his horn into the fountain. According to the medieval legend, the horn of the unicorn could absorb poison. If a stream were poisoned by an evil serpent, the unicorn purified the water with his horn so that the animals and birds could safely drink.

51

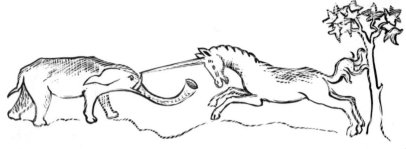

Many people believed such stories in the Middle Ages, for much of the world was still mysterious and unexplored. The few men who ventured to distant lands often brought back tales of strange beasts, and even the great traveler Marco Polo declared he had seen a unicorn in the East. The animal had one horn on its head, but otherwise it did not look at all as he had expected. What Marco Polo saw was probably a rhinoceros!

The graceful unicorn of the tapestries is finally killed after a hard fight and carried in triumph to a castle on the edge of the forest. The designer of the tapestries must have watched hunting parties like this one, bringing home a stag or a wild boar. His hunters look like real people. He knew all about their dress, their weapons and their hounds—short-nosed mastiffs and slender greyhounds. The weaver, with wonderful skill, has reproduced every detail, down to the brocade patterns on the men's doublets. The forest is just as carefully pictured, and in the seven tapestries there are more than a hundred different kinds of flowers.

52

Medieval people were very fond of flowers, as we know from the frequent descriptions of gardens in stories and poems of those days. Castles often had flower gardens, and in the winter, *mille-fleurs* or "thousand-flower" tapestries made a never-fading garden indoors. There were many other subjects for tapestries. Some simply had a repeating pattern showing the coat of arms of their owner; others illustrated romances or stories from the Bible; but whatever their subject might be, tapestries gave the rooms color and warmth and formed a rich background for the simple, solid furniture.

SNIPE, WILD DUCK,
PARTRIDGES AND HUNTER

from the third and fourth
Unicorn Tapestries

FURNITURE

HESTS WERE FOUND IN EVERY MEDIEVAL castle. They were the commonest furniture, so useful and important that they were made by special craftsmen known as "cofferers," from "coffer," the old word for chest. Clothes, linens, tapestries and jewelry were all stored in chests, and the flat lids served equally well as benches, tables or beds. Noble households were constantly on the move, as we have seen, and chests were used as trunks for their belongings and carried from castle to castle by pack horse or wagon.

The earliest chests were true "trunks," made from sections of hollowed-out tree trunks. Then rough boxes were constructed of hand-hewn planks joined

54

together with wooden pegs, until in the thirteenth century the cofferers began to make really beautiful chests. The planks were cut thinner and fitted into grooves in four thick corner slabs, called stiles, which you can see on the oak chest opposite. Great oak forests flourished in medieval Europe, and oak, hard and enduring, was the usual wood for furniture. It was good for carving, and on the fronts and sides of chests we find rows of delicate pointed arches, figures of saints and tournament scenes, carved in relief. Now dark with age, these were probably colored and gilded when they were new, and the Italian *cassoni*, or marriage chests, designed to hold the dowry of a bride, were adorned with large paintings.

STORING JEWELS IN A CHEST
*from Queen Mary's
Psalter*

CASSONE, OR
MARRIAGE CHEST
Italian, about 1450

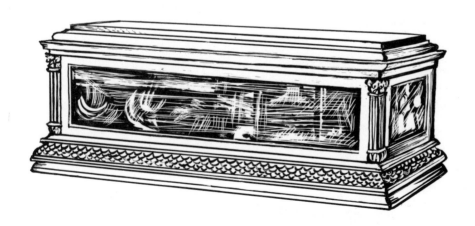

OAK CUPBOARD
English, 15th century

**LONG BENCH,
OR SETTLE**

CARVED FLOWERS
*from the Italian
chair*

When the simple chest was set on legs and made to open in front instead of on top, it became a cupboard like this one. Cupboards were common in the fifteenth century, and some were very large. Chairs were rare in the medieval household and were used only by important people. Lesser folk stood up in the presence of their lord or sat on benches and stools. The chair was a sign of authority, and even today a chairman presides over a meeting and remarks are addressed to the chair.

The ornate Italian chair opposite developed from the humble three-legged stool. The French chair is simply a chest with the sides and back extended, but it shows us a new kind of construction—paneling—which was very important in the making of furniture.

56

OAK CHAIR
French,
15th century

OAK CHAIR
Italian,
15th century

To make a chair like this one the craftsman first built a framework of squared timbers and then filled it in with thin boards or panels. He fitted the panels into grooves in the framework, and unlike the thick planks used in the old style of construction, the panels had room to shrink or swell without splitting. The uprights and crosspieces of the framework were held together by mortise-and-tenon joints, in which tongues of wood fitted into slots. Furniture joined in this way was made by "joiners"; carpenters did the rougher work, fastened with nails or pegs.

Chests and cupboards were made with the same

57

LINENFOLD PANELING
from the French chair

PRIVATE BEDROOM WITH FIREPLACE *from Queen Mary's Psalter*

paneled construction and were generally decorated with variations of the popular "linenfold" pattern, which you can see on the panels of the chair. Paneled woodwork was also used for screens and for lining the walls of small rooms. A private bedroom, particularly with a fireplace, was a rare luxury in the Middle Ages. A number of people usually shared a room, and the more elaborate beds were hung with curtains which could be drawn at night for warmth and privacy. Servants and less important guests had no proper beds but slept in the castle hall, stretched out on chests and benches.

The hall was the center of the medieval castle, and here the whole household took their meals, the servants at long tables in the main part of the hall and the lord and lady on the raised dais at one end.

58

CASTLE HALL

The tables were not well-made pieces of furniture but broad boards laid on trestles. They could be cleared away after meals to make room for games and dancing, or more tables could be put up if unexpected guests arrived. Hospitality was generous in the Middle Ages. The rough tables were spread with lavish meals and the tableware used by the lord and his special guests was beautiful to see.

59

POTTERY VASE
Italian, 15th century

BRONZE AQUAEMANALES
Above, German, about 1400
Right, French or German,
15th century

TABLEWARE

HE GUESTS OF A KNIGHT OR NOBLEMAN
were furnished with cups and plates,
knives and spoons. Forks were sometimes used, as early as the thirteenth
century, but only for fruits and
pastries. Before the meal began, a page brought in
a jug of scented water and a bowl for the guests to
wash their hands. His bronze jug or aquaemanale
might be shaped like an animal with the waterspout
projecting from its chest. A knight on horseback was
a favorite design and was even imitated in pottery for
those who could not afford bronze.

POTTERY JUG
Italian, 15th century

MAJOLICA VASE
Italian,
15th century

LUSTERWARE DISH
Spanish,
15th century

Medieval pottery was mostly cheap and crude, but beautiful earthenware from Italy and Spain was displayed with pride in castle halls. The Mohammedans had brought to Europe the art of making fine pottery, and in Spain throughout the Middle Ages they produced their famous lusterware. This Moorish pottery had an iridescent shine because of the metallic film on the surface of the glaze, and was decorated with animals, birds and leaf patterns. It was made also on the island of Majorca, off the coast of Spain; and Italians, trading and fighting with the Moors of Majorca, took some lusterware back to Italy where it inspired their own craftsmen, particularly in Florence, to make the handsome painted pottery known as majolica.

Large earthenware beer mugs came from Germany, where beer was the usual drink. In England

61

EARTHENWARE BEER MUG
German, 14th century

SILVER WINE CUP
*English, 15th
century*

SERVING FOOD
WITH MUSIC

ordinary people preferred home-brewed ale, and the rich drank French and Italian wines from silver wine-cups. Cheaper wooden cups, often of maple wood, were called mazers, from the old name for maple. This one has good advice engraved on its silver rim:

MAZER, OR WOODEN CUP
English, 14th century

> Hold your tongue and say the best,
> And let your neighbors sit in rest,
> Whoso listeth God to please,
> Let his neighbor live in ease.

Plates, or trenchers, for meat were often crusty slices of "trencher bread" which could be eaten after use or thrown to the waiting dogs around the table. Stews and puddings were eaten from wooden or pewter plates, but on the nobleman's table there were plates of silver and gold. One of the most elaborate vessels was the saltcellar, usually in the shape of a ship, and its position on the table determined the

ROASTING ON A SPIT

62

FEASTING

seating of the guests. Noble guests sat "above the salt," and more humble ones below.

This ivory-handled knife was used to serve out slices of meat onto the plates of the guests. One of the duties of a squire was to carve the meat at his lord's table. It might be a great joint of roast beef or a suckling pig, a haunch of venison or a dish of wild duck. On state occasions a roasted swan or a peacock was brought to the table, resplendent in all its feathers. Tiny songbirds were cooked on spits or baked in spicy pies, and fish, fresh or salted, was always eaten on Fridays and through Lent.

The pictures of feasting and kitchen work come from the two Psalters which have already given us glimpses of how people lived, and it is time now to look more closely at these and other books, once treasured possessions in medieval castles.

SERVING KNIFE
Italian,
14th century

CREATION OF THE ANIMALS
from Queen Mary's Psalter

BOOKS FOR THE CASTLE

 N THE MIDDLE AGES MOST BOOKS BE-
longed to churches, monasteries and
schools. It was rare to find a library
in a castle. The earliest printed
books did not appear until the
fifteenth century, and before then all books were
copied by hand and were costly to buy. At first
they were made only by monks, but later the work
was taken up by growing numbers of craftsmen out-
side the Church. They had their workshops in towns
or traveled about to monasteries and castles where
they made books to order. Rich people who could
afford to buy books were not content with plain, un-
adorned manuscripts, copied by capable scribes.
They wanted their books to be works of art, lavishly
decorated by skilled painters with colored capital
letters and glowing miniatures; and among the loveliest medieval manuscripts are the Books of Psalms,
or Psalters, made for kings, queens and nobles.

Queen Mary's Psalter takes its name from Mary

GROTESQUE DECORATIONS
from the Luttrell
Psalter

Tudor, Queen of England, who was given the book in 1553, but the Psalter was made more than two hundred years earlier for an English nobleman. The first owner of the Luttrell Psalter was a knight of Lincolnshire, Sir Geoffrey Luttrell, whose picture is included in his book.

Both Psalters are filled with glorious pictures and contain far more than just the Psalms. The drawing of the Creation of the Animals from Queen Mary's Psalter is one of a series telling Old Testament stories up to the death of Solomon. Then there are scenes from the life of Christ and a calendar of holy days illustrated with a seasonal picture for each month—hawking in May, cutting grain in August, butchering pigs in December.

We have already seen drawings of everyday life from both books. In the Luttrell Psalter these are mingled with a whole menagerie of grotesque and

A LOADED CART
ON A STEEP HILL
from the Luttrell Psalter

fantastic beings, half human, half animal. Medieval artists loved to draw such creatures. We find some of them in Queen Mary's Psalter too, but in this book there are also lively drawings of birds and beasts which make up a complete bestiary, all in pictures.

Bestiaries, or natural-history books, were popular reading in the Middle Ages. Their descriptions of animals, including fabulous beasts like the unicorn, were a mixture of accurate observation, scraps of old legend and a good portion of stern moral teaching. The whale, in the picture below, was said to rest on the top of the sea until green grass grew on its back. Sailors camped there, thinking it an island, but when the whale felt the heat of their fire, it dived and drowned them.

Books of Hours, like Psalters, gave painters a wonderful chance for rich decoration. These were private prayer books with the prayers arranged for the

THE WHALE
from Queen Mary's Psalter

67

INITIAL LETTER
*from the Hours of Jeanne d'Evreux,
French, 14th century*

eight canonical hours of the day, from Matins in the early morning to Compline at night. They were more personal and intimate than the great Psalters. *The Hours of Jeanne D'Evreux* is a tiny book less than four inches high and was probably ordered by Queen Jeanne as a gift for her husband, King Charles IV of France. The small exquisite pictures, drawn almost entirely in black and white, are the work of Jean Pucelle, a well-known French illuminator and the head of a busy workshop in Paris. Besides illustrating books with miniatures, Pucelle liked to surround the pages of text with decorative frames of leaves and flowers, birds and butterflies. This became a fashion with the French illuminators, and their Books of Hours were famous for the brilliance of their flowery borders.

One of the most beautiful of these books was copied and illuminated in 1492 for Queen Anne of

68

Here and opposite,
GARDEN PLANTS
*painted by Jean Bourdichon
in a Book of Hours,
Early 16th century*

Brittany who was specially fond of flowers. The Unicorn Tapestries, also made for Queen Anne, were full of flowers, as we have seen, and in the borders of her Book of Hours the painter Jean Bourdichon presented her with a complete medieval garden. The plants in his paintings are as realistic as those in the tapestries, and even the insects perched on the leaves seem to be drawn from life.

Almost every flower and fruit he painted, from the cucumber to the rose, had its uses, both as a medicine and as a food. The castle garden was very important, and the secrets of good gardening were explained in a book which must have been widely read by knights and nobles. This was *The Book of Rural Profits*, written in the fourteenth century by Petrus Crescentius of Bologna, giving detailed directions for the wise management of country estates. In a fifteenth-century copy we find a picture of an ideal garden

with neat beds of small fruit trees and green vegetables for salad.

Another popular book was *The Book of Hawking, Hunting and Heraldry*, printed in 1486. This was one of the earliest books published by William Caxton, the first printer in England. Ten years later a new edition appeared with a chapter on fishing, illustrated with this woodcut picture.

By the time of Caxton, the new art of printing had spread all over Europe from Germany where it be-

FISHERMAN
*from The Book of
Hawking, Hunting
and Heraldry,
English, 15th century*

gan. Manuscripts were still being copied in the old
way, but books of every kind could be bought in
printed editions. There were books of poetry and
romance, histories like the great *Nuremberg Chron-
icle* with its hundreds of woodcuts, and travel books
describing the marvels of distant lands. But religious
books outnumbered all the rest. Now that they were
cheaper to buy, more and more people wanted vol-
umes of Psalms and prayers and the stories of saints.
This was still the Age of Faith, and from birth to
death, people's lives centered around their church,
whether it was a great cathedral in a town, a tiny
church in a country village or the private chapel of
a castle.

PRINTING PRESS

Diptychs and Reliquaries

I N MANY CASTLES THERE WAS A PRIVATE
chapel for the lord and lady and
their household, and often on the
altar stood small ivory statues and
little panels carved in relief. Ivory
ranked with gold and silver as a precious material,
suitable for the making of sacred things. For hundreds of years it could only be brought to Europe in
the form of elephant tusks from Africa and India.
Then in the ninth century the restless Vikings discovered Iceland, and sailing on to Greenland, they
found herds of walruses along the western coast. The
Vikings hunted the huge beasts for their tough hide
which made strong rigging for ships, and above all,
for their fine ivory tusks. Cargoes of walrus ivory
from Greenland were shipped across the stormy sea

**IVORY FIGURE OF
THE VIRGIN AND CHILD**
French, 14th century

Above, SHEPHERD
WITH BAGPIPES
from the diptych

to Europe and were accepted as a fine substitute for the rare tusks from the East.

IVORY DIPTYCH
French, 14th century

Looking at ivory statues, like this small Virgin and Child, you will often find them shaped to the natural curve of the tusk, either of walrus or elephant. Ivory panels were hinged together in pairs or in sets of three to make diptychs and triptychs which could be closed up and easily carried about. This little diptych, with its carvings of the Nativity and the Crucifixion, is like many which were made in the fourteenth century. Originally painted in bright colors, these two small reliefs remind us of minia-

73

SHEPHERD AND HIS DOG
from the Hours of Jeanne d'Evreux

tures in a Book of Hours. The ivory carver may have taken book illustrations as his models, for he had to obey strict rules and traditions when carving scenes from the life of Christ and could not portray them just as he pleased.

Another Christmas scene, coupled with a picture of the Resurrection, appears on this tiny diptych of silver gilt and enamel. In the Resurrection, Christ is shown stepping out of the open tomb while the Roman guards lie asleep in the foreground. Like the

designer of the Nine Heroes Tapestries, the artist has dressed his Roman soldiers in the armor of his own day, complete with conical basinets on their heads. The soldiers are much smaller than the figure of Christ; the most important figure in a medieval picture is often drawn larger than the rest.

Small diptychs were frequently worn as pendants on gold neck chains. Pendants were a favorite kind of jewelry in the fifteenth century and included elaborate locket reliquaries like this one with a brilliant enameled picture of Christ appearing to Saint Dominic. These pendants were made to open and to hold some small relic from the body of a saint—perhaps a wisp of hair or a fragment of bone.

The relics of saints were very much revered.

MAN WEARING A PENDANT
Wood sculpture, Flemish,
15th century

People went on long pilgrimages to churches where saints were buried or relics preserved. For those who could not make the great pilgrimages to Rome and Jerusalem there were many other shrines to visit nearer at hand. The pilgrim on the left wears a scallop shell in his hat to show that he has journeyed to the shrine of Saint James at Compostella in Spain.

Geoffrey Chaucer, in his book *The Canterbury Tales*, has given us a vivid description of a large and cheerful band of pilgrims setting out from London on a fresh April morning in the fourteenth century. They were bound for the shrine of Saint Thomas à Becket at Canterbury, the most famous shrine in England. At the end of their journey they would see wonders beyond belief. Under the lofty vaults of the cathedral the tomb of the saint was ablaze with gold, jewels and enamels, the gifts of kings and nobles; and all around it were displayed the richest treasures of the cathedral, the glorious work of craftsmen for the Church.

PILGRIM WITH HIS
STAFF AND WALLET
*from the Luttrell
Psalter*

METAL FIGURE OF
THOMAS À BECKET
*Pilgrim's badge
from Canterbury*

PART II

Things made for the church

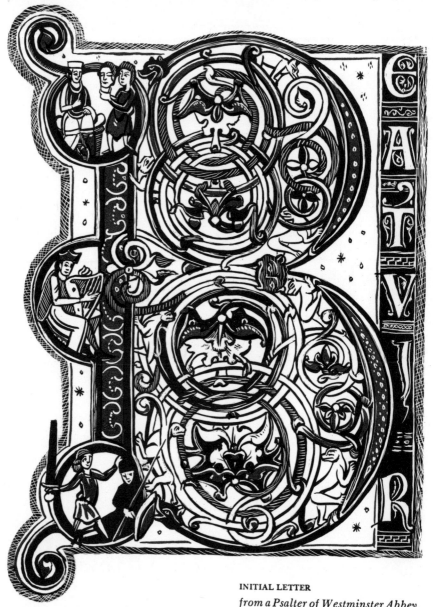

INITIAL LETTER
*from a Psalter of Westminster Abbey,
late 12th century*

Books for the church

ATE IN THE TWELFTH CENTURY, WHEN knights were fighting in the Third Crusade, a painter at the Abbey of Westminster made this wonderful capital letter for the first page of a Psalter. The Latin text of the First Psalm begins with the words *Beatus vir* ("Blessed is the man"), and the illuminator was expected to lavish his finest decorations on this "Beatus" page. In the Psalter of Westminster, he carried out his design in gold and brilliant colors and adorned the letter "B" with little scenes from the life of King David.

At the time this Psalter was finished, monks were still the chief makers of books. In most monasteries

79

books were copied in a scriptorium, or writing room, where the scribes kept a·strict rule of silence, speaking to each other only by signs. They made books for their own monastery, for cathedrals and parish churches and for the libraries of scholars.

The Church had been the home of learning ever since the fall of the Roman Empire in the fifth century A.D. All through the Dark Ages, when western Europe was overrun by fierce barbarian invaders, the Church kept the light of learning alive. Bibles and Gospel Books and the works of the early Christian fathers were preserved in monasteries, and the monks even copied the writings of pagan Roman authors.

Some of the loveliest books they made were used in the daily services of the Church. The monks worshipped in church at each of the canonical hours of the day, beginning at midnight when they were roused from bed to attend Matins and Lauds before dawn.

The capital "D," with its miniature of singing monks, comes from a great volume of church music for the guidance of the choir. This manuscript was made in Italy about twenty years after the publication of the first and most famous of all printed books, the Gutenberg Bible of 1456. Many of the early printed books, like the great Bible, were meant to be used in churches, but there was still a need for manuscripts. Long after the invention of printing, the scribes and illuminators, both monks and laymen, continued to produce books by the same methods they had followed for centuries.

The first step in making a manuscript was the preparation of the parchment. Paper was not widely used for books until the invention of printing when it was found to be the best material to print on.

INITIAL AND BORDER
*from a music manuscript,
Italian, 13th or 14th
century*

Sheepskins for parchment, or calfskins for vellum, had to be soaked, stretched and scraped, then dusted with chalk and rubbed smooth with pumice.

The scribe was given folded sheets, cut to the size of the book and arranged in sets of four leaves. To guide his writing he ruled lines on the pages with a blunt tool which left little grooves in the parchment. He made his own writing ink from lampblack, charcoal or the bark of thorn trees. His pen was a goose quill, cut square at the tip to form the thick and thin strokes of the medieval script. As the scribe copied the text, he left spaces for capital letters and miniatures, and when the writing was done, the pages were passed on to the painter for decoration.

This miniature showing Christ rising from the
tomb is the work of a German artist, but it is very
like the picture on the tiny silver diptych of English
workmanship on page 74. The figures are painted
against a gold background which represented, to the
medieval artist, the shining light of heaven.

Gold was used increasingly in manuscripts from
the twelfth century on. It could be ground to powder
and made into a paint, but the effect of gold leaf was

far more brilliant. The metal was beaten into leaves so thin that the painter had to hold his breath when he touched them, for fear of blowing them away. It was a delicate task to stick the gold to the parchment. There were various recipes for a good glue, including white of egg and a jelly made by boiling scraps of vellum. Having fixed the gold firmly in place, the painter polished it with a stone or a wild boar's tooth, and sometimes he pricked little designs into the metal to make it sparkle.

The cover of a manuscript had to be worthy of the glowing pages within. Some books were given plain, practical bindings of wooden boards covered with deer- or sheepskin, but books to be used in a great church often had covers of the finest metalwork. This splendid book cover of gilded copper with designs of angels in champlevé enamel was made at Limoges, in France, and decorated by the same technique as the enameled pendant on page 39.

Small ivory panels, like those in diptychs, were frequently set into the book covers and surrounded by borders of large round-cut gems. On the panel over the page are carvings of a man, a lion, an ox and an eagle. These symbols, which appear again

METAL BOOK COVER
French, 13th century

and again in church art, stand for the writers of the four Gospels—Matthew, Mark, Luke and John.

Some books were bound in embroidered cloth. The embroiderer's art ranked high in the Middle Ages and was closely linked with bookmaking, for painters of miniatures also made drawings for embroidery. We have seen how lavishly the clothes of knights and ladies were decorated with needlework. This art was even more important in the adornment of vestments for priests, and the embroiderers produced their greatest masterpieces in the service of the Church.

CHRIST IN MAJESTY
Ivory panel
from a book cover,
German, 11th or
12th century

ADORATION OF THE MAGI
from an embroidered
chasuble, English,
14th century

EMBROIDERY

RICHLY EMBROIDERED VESTMENTS, gleaming with gold and gems, added grandeur and dignity to the ceremonies of the Church. Even small country churches had a few elaborate vestments for their priests; and in the treasuries of great cathedrals there were scores of these embroideries, often the gifts of kings or the work of noble ladies in castles. Many vestments were destroyed when they were old and worn, but enough have survived to give us some idea of the glory of medieval church needlework.

The picture of the Adoration of the Magi is sewn

87

BISHOP WEARING A CHASUBLE
Ivory chessman,
12th century

SAINT MICHAEL AND
THE DRAGON
*from the Syon Cope,
English, 13th century*

BISHOP WEARING A COPE
*from the tapestry of
The Christian Heroes,
14th century*

in threads of silk and gold on a red velvet chasuble, the vestment worn by the priest at Mass. This chasuble is English work, which was famous throughout Europe in the thirteenth and fourteenth centuries and known everywhere by its Latin name, *opus anglicanum.* The making of these embroideries took months of patient toil. Monks and nuns did much of the work, but as the demand for vestments increased, guilds of professional embroiderers were formed, both for men and women.

The embroiderers excelled in the decoration of copes, the long cloaks worn by the clergy in processions. These could be made of silk, velvet, satin or even cloth of gold, and were not only embroidered with religious pictures but also with designs of eagles

88

and griffins, fishes, tigers and oak leaves, or pomegranates and roses worked in pearls.

The warlike figure of Saint Michael slaying the dragon, a favorite subject after the time of the Crusades, comes from the Syon Cope which shows us English work at its finest. Such splendid vestments as this were worn by the English clergy who visited Rome in 1246, and the Pope was so impressed that he ordered similar vestments for himself.

The Syon Cope is made from a double thickness of linen, completely covered with stitching in gold, silver and colored silks. Scenes from the life of Christ and the Virgin and figures of saints are enclosed, like Saint Michael, in red quatrefoil shapes, outlined in gold, and the green spaces between them are filled with beautiful six-winged angels.

The most important subjects are grouped on the back of the cope where the material falls from the shoulders of the wearer and the embroidery can best be seen. The Crucifixion is in the center, worked in silver on a gold ground. Originally there were figures of the Twelve Apostles around the edges of the cope, but these were cut off and replaced later by borders of shields and coats of arms.

The embroiderers used chain stitch and other simple stitches when working on the figures. If you look closely at the faces in the English work, you will

89

ANGEL
from the Syon Cope

SAINT CATHERINE
*from a German
religious tapestry,
14th century*

see how the lines of stitching go around in circles on the cheeks. Sometimes the cheeks were pushed out from behind with a heated metal knob to raise them in relief. The solid color of the backgrounds on the Syon Cope was made by couching. The red or green silks were laid flat on the linen and fastened in place with linen thread, a method which produces a lovely satinlike effect.

These wonderful vestments matched the great churches of the Middle Ages in the richness of their decoration. The walls of the churches were covered with embroidered hangings and tapestries or painted with large pictures illustrating the lives of saints or stories from the Bible. The embroiderers made altar cloths, like the one in the miniature opposite, and to screen the altars there were curtains worked with the figures of saints. The windows were filled with pictures in glowing stained glass; the intricate carvings of church furniture and statuary were painted and gilded, and from the tiled floors to the lofty vaulting, the church interiors blazed with color.

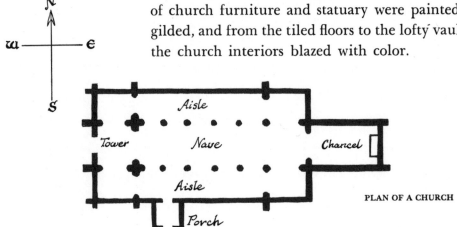

PLAN OF A CHURCH

ᙍOOD CARVING

HE FURNITURE OF A CHURCH WAS
mostly at the east end, near the high
altar. There were rarely any pews
or benches in the nave for the
people to sit on. In England, pews
came into use in the fifteenth century when prosper-
ous wool merchants spent much of their wealth on
building and repairing churches. With a liking for
comfort, they installed whole sets of benches, often
beautifully carved. Otherwise people stood during

Above, CELEBRATION
OF MASS IN A CHURCH
*from an Italian
manuscript, 14th
century*

**STALL WITH SEAT
TURNED DOWN**

**CHOIR STALL WITH SEAT
TURNED UP SHOWING MISERICORD**
*French,
15th century*

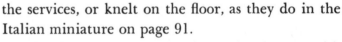

the services, or knelt on the floor, as they do in the Italian miniature on page 91.

Behind the priest in this picture is a lectern with an open book on it. These tall bookstands were usually carved in the shape of an eagle with spread wings. The great book of music for the singers was placed on a lectern in the middle of the choir, and a second lectern stood at the north side of the altar to hold the book for the Gospel reading at Mass.

High-backed seats, sometimes with ornate wooden canopies, were placed in the chancel for priests and bishops; and in cathedrals and large parish churches

LECTERN
*French,
15th century*

CARVED MISERICORD
English, 15th century

there were also stalls for the choir. The choristers had to stand for such long hours that the medieval carpenters took pity on them and designed a special kind of stall to give them some relief. The seat tipped up and had a little ledge underneath it on which the singer could sit or lean and still look as though he were standing. The ledge was called a misericord, from the Latin word for pity, and misericords were decorated with some of the liveliest carving of the Middle Ages.

Here a wood carver has made a portrait of himself at work, chiseling out the delicate tracery of a screen. He has three apprentices to help him and a little dog to lie at his feet, while in the scrolls at the sides are a saw and chisel, tools of his craft.

93

MAN SINGING
*Carved on the arm
of the French choir stall*

DOG HOWLING
Carved on the arm
of the French choir stall

The making of a set of choir stalls was directed by a master carpenter. The carvers of the misericords worked under the master for a few pennies a day, and as their work was hidden under the seats, they were left to carve what they pleased.

They carved knights jousting, a game of football, jesters and dancers, a hunter after a hare, and a man warming his toes by the fire. Sometimes they illustrated Bible stories and saints' legends, but they often used scenes from romances, especially the tale of sly Reynard, the fox. They also liked to carve animals and birds taken from the bestiaries, and they borrowed ideas from the picture calendars in Psalters and Books of Hours which showed work on the farm. The carver of this harvest scene has even

CARVED MISERICORD
English, 15th century

ANGEL WITH A LUTE
from a carved
choir stall,
15th century

added two grotesque monsters like those in the Luttrell Psalter.

Carvings of small comical people and animals appear unexpectedly on the armrests of choir stalls, but we also find such lovely figures as this angel playing the lute. The calm and peaceful Italian angel holds a candlestick and might have stood on an altar.

Besides the high altar at the east end of the church there were smaller altars which were placed in separate side chapels if the building were large. The church was known by the name of its patron saint, but the side chapels were dedicated to different saints and usually contained their statues, carved in wood or stone.

95

ANGEL WITH A CANDLESTICK
Italian, 15th century

Saint Ambrose, one of the Fathers of the early church, is shown in the vestments of a bishop. Like the statue of the Virgin and Child, the carving of Saint Ambrose was originally painted. Furniture and sculpture were as brightly colored as the whole interior of the church. Their decoration was one of the many tasks of the painters whose craft was in such great demand in the Middle Ages.

VIRGIN AND CHILD
French, 13th century

96

paintings

EDIEVAL PAINTERS SPREAD COLOR
everywhere, indoors and out. Only
scholars and rich people could en-
joy the miniatures in manuscripts,
but anyone walking the streets of a
town could see the gaily-painted decorations of
houses and churches. Anyone could admire the
splendor of painted banners, shields and saddles
when knights rode abroad; and even the poorest

SAINT CHRISTOPHER
*from a Spanish
altarpiece, 1480*

people, when they came to church, could gaze at the Virgin and Child and the saints on the tall panels of a painted altarpiece.

Although most of their pictures were painted for churches, the artists were generally laymen and members of the painters' guild. The painters in a town sometimes formed a guild with the druggists or the goldsmiths, or even with the sword forgers, tapestry weavers, carvers, potters and saddlers. It seems strange to us to include painters, some of them men of genius, in a company of craftsmen; but even the greatest artists were craftsmen, just as much as the goldsmiths and the potters. Their pictures would not have lasted to the present day if they had not followed the strict rules of craftsmanship laid down by the heads of their guild.

The painter's craft was difficult and took a long time to learn. Apart from wall paintings, pictures were done on wooden panels, and the artist had to know how to prepare the panel for his work. The wood had to be aged and seasoned so that it would not warp; and for a large panel several planks were fastened together with a strong glue made from cheese and lime. Then the wood was coated with several layers of gesso, a mixture of glue and powdered chalk. Only when this was dry and rubbed as smooth as ivory was the surface fit for paint.

PAINTER'S APPRENTICE
GRINDING COLORS ON
A SLAB OF MARBLE

PAINTER AT WORK

98

The colors were not bought ready-made, and medieval artists traveled far and wide to find the best ingredients and recipes for making their paints. There were vegetable dyes, such as the reds and blues made from madder and woad; and there were natural earth colors—yellow ocher, red-brown sienna, white chalk and the green earth known as *terra verde*. White lead was also used by painters; verdigris from copper produced green; and red was made from cinnabar, the ore of mercury. Medieval pictures are gay with red, for it was plentiful and easy to get, but the best ultramarine blue was rare and expensive. This was the precious mineral, lapis lazuli, brought by camel caravan from distant eastern mines near the source of the river Oxus.

The colors were ground to powder and mixed with gum and water to make water color, or with white of egg to make the opaque tempera paint which was commonly used for panel pictures. Painters seldom mixed their colors with oil until the fifteenth century. Then the great Flemish painter, Jan Van Eyck, began to work in a new way. Van Eyck would make a drawing on a wood panel with the usual egg tempera, but over this he painted in oils, laying on the color in thin, transparent glazes. You can see his pictures today with their colors still fresh, alive and glowing.

99

ANGEL PLAYING A VIOL
from a Spanish altarpiece,
15th century

Van Eyck painted portraits as well as religious pictures. Portrait painting was a new art in the fifteenth century and was growing more popular, especially in the cities of Italy and Flanders. When a merchant or a nobleman paid for the making of an altarpiece for a church, a portrait of himself, as the donor, was often worked into the design. If the altarpiece were a triptych, with the Virgin and Child in the central panel, the donor and his whole family might be shown kneeling in prayer among the figures of saints on the two side panels.

A painted altarpiece, or retable, formed a wonderful background of color for the altar, but in the fourteenth century there was a great new enthusiasm for retables of carved alabaster, and the "alabaster-men" who made them soon became some of the busiest craftsmen in Europe.

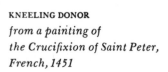

KNEELING DONOR
*from a painting of
the Crucifixion of Saint Peter,
French, 1451*

100

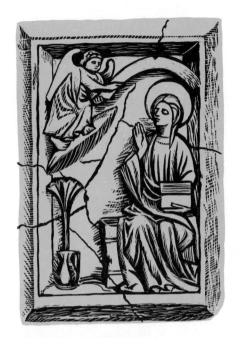

CARVINGS IN ALABASTER

IN THE LATE MIDDLE AGES GREAT QUANtities of alabaster carvings were made in England. The stone was quarried not far from the town of Nottingham. Little statues of saints and carvings in relief, made by the alabastermen of Nottingham, were sent to churches all over the country, where groups of the carved panels—five, seven or more—were set into painted wooden frames to make large or small altarpieces.

ALABASTER PANEL OF
THE ANNUNCIATION
English,
14th century

101

SAINT CHRISTOPHER
English,
15th century

THOMAS À BECKET
LANDING IN ENGLAND
English, 15th century

Many of these panels were shipped across the Channel to France, to Germany and Italy, and even northwest to Iceland. They illustrated scenes from the New Testament, the life of the Virgin and the legends of saints. The little carved figures acted out the stories in a simple way that anyone could understand, and they were painted in gay colors which helped to make the meaning plain. Saints could be told by their golden hair and halos, while wicked men had tawny-red faces and hair of raven black.

The panel on the left is a scene from the life of Saint Thomas à Becket whose shrine was such a famous place of pilgrimage. Clad in his cope and miter as Archbishop of Canterbury, he is shown here arriving in England from France where he had been exiled after his quarrel with the English king, Henry II. The people welcomed him home, but before many days had passed Thomas à Becket was murdered in his own cathedral by four of the King's knights.

With the production of so many of these little panels, the carving became careless and hasty, but this fine statue of Saint Christopher shows what the alabastermen could do at their best. The tiny figure of the donor, who presented the statue to a church, kneels in prayer at the feet of the saint, and the whole sculpture has the same spirit of devotion that we find in the carved ivories.

SAINT FIACRE, PATRON
SAINT OF GARDENERS
English, 15th century

CREATION OF THE ANIMALS
Italian, 11th century

CARVINGS IN IVORY

RARE AND PRECIOUS IVORY, FINELY carved, had its place in the church as well as in the castle. Ivory diptychs, triptychs and small statues were displayed in churches, as they were in the private chapels of the wealthy, and we have already seen how panels of ivory were used on the covers of books. This small panel, with its lively picture of the Creation of the Animals, was once part of the front of an altar in the cathedral of Salerno in Italy, but it may have been carved originally to decorate the throne of a bishop.

The intricate carving above formed the head of a bishop's staff, known as a tau cross because it was T-shaped at the top like the letter *tau* of the Greek alphabet. This carving is English work and very different from the Italian relief. Cutting deeply into the ivory, the carver has made a vivid pattern of lights and shadows, and he has used the same writhing and intertwining shapes as we saw in the illuminated letter "B" from the Psalter of Westminster, made in the same century. On either side of the Virgin and Child are energetic figures struggling with serpents. More than mere decorations, these are the medieval artist's way of picturing the endless battle between Good and Evil, between the Church and Satan.

The serpent was not always a symbol of evil. It also represented the prudence and wisdom so neces-

105

sary for the bishop. He was supposed, above all, to be a good shepherd to his people, and in the early Middle Ages a decorative version of the shepherd's crook replaced the tau cross as a design for the heads of bishops' staffs, or croziers.

The simple crozier head opposite is carved in the form of a single coiled serpent, but sometimes a figure, or a whole group of figures, appears inside the curve of the crook. In this ornate crozier of a later date, the figure of Christ enthroned in majesty is actually two figures, seated back to back, so that the carving looks equally impressive from both sides.

Such beautiful croziers could be admired by many

HEAD OF A BISHOP'S STAFF
Italian, 14th century

106

Opposite, CROZIER HEAD
OF CHAMPLEVÉ ENAMEL
WITH SAINT MICHAEL AND
THE DRAGON
French, 13th century

IVORY PYX
French, 14th century

when the bishop walked in a religious procession in his magnificent vestments; but very few people ever saw the tiny reliefs of scenes from the life of the Virgin carved on this small ivory pyx. Originally covered by a lid, the pyx held the consecrated bread, and the priest carried it with him when he went to administer Communion to the sick.

Vessels designed for such sacred uses were masterpieces of medieval craftsmanship and filled the treasuries of churches with untold splendor and loveliness. Many of the craftsmen must have been monks, and like the carver of the pyx, they labored not for their own gain, nor to give pleasure to other men, but to glorify God.

107

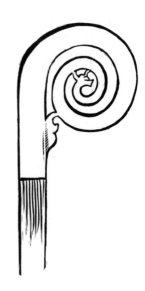

IVORY CROZIER HEAD
Italian, 12th century

TREASURES OF THE CHURCH

ANY OF THE GREATEST TREASURES OF the Church were made by the craftsmen of Limoges, the town in France so famous for its enamel workers. This beautiful pyx in the form of a dove, the symbol of the Holy Ghost, is made of gilded copper and champlevé enamel. The back of the dove is hinged to open like a lid, and the wings and tail have a feather pattern of enamel inlay in blue, white and green.

This kind of pyx was meant to be hung from a chain in front of the altar. On the altar itself stood the cross and a pair of candlesticks. They were usu-

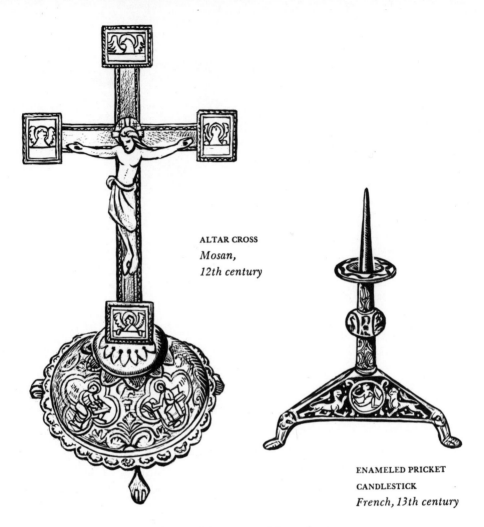

ALTAR CROSS
Mosan,
12th century

ENAMELED PRICKET
CANDLESTICK
French, 13th century

ally pricket candlesticks like this one, with a long
spike to pierce and hold a fat candle of beeswax.

The altar cross is Mosan work, made by a craftsman in the valley of the river Meuse in the duchy

THE BERTINUS CHALICE
French, 1222

PATEN
German, 13th century

of Lorraine. The goldsmiths of this district were as famous in the twelfth and thirteenth centuries as the enamel workers of Limoges. Around the base of the cross are enameled pictures of the four Evangelists, Matthew, Mark, Luke and John, with their symbols—the man, the lion, the ox and the eagle.

In the treasuries of great churches were many vessels needed for the celebration of Mass, some for everyday use and more elaborate ones for festivals.

The chalice for the wine and the paten for the bread were usually made as a pair with matching decorations. The Bertinus chalice is named after its maker, the monk, Brother Bertinus, who engraved his name and the date, 1222, around the base. The

110

silver cup, gilded within, is quite plain in shape to make it easy to clean and polish. The only decoration is the design of animals and plants twined around the knob of the stem, the handgrip by which the chalice was held. The jeweled paten belongs to a more ornate set and is engraved with pictures of Christ, a saint and two Old Testament figures.

Two graceful altar cruets held the water and wine for the service. The enameled bowl was for washing the hands of the priest, and the wonderful bronze dragon is a water jug, or aquaemanale. The water was poured into the bowl from the dragon's mouth, while the tail, curled over the creature's back, formed a convenient handle.

The metalworkers made these aquaemanales in all kinds of exciting animal shapes. Their bronze

ALTAR CRUET
French, 13th century

BRONZE AQUAEMANALE
German, 12th or 13th century

ENAMELED BOWL
French, 13th century

SAMSON AND THE LION
German aquaemanale,
14th century

was a mixture of zinc and copper which could be polished until it shone like gold. The molten metal was poured into a mold to get the general shape of the sculpture, but the finishing was done by hand and details like the scales of the dragon were carved in the cold metal.

Also cast in bronze is this egg-shaped incense burner, or censer, which was carried by a server during the ceremonies at the altar. A censer very like this one can be seen in the little picture opposite, which is part of the decoration of a reliquary.

Every church possessed at least a few relics of saints, and great numbers of reliquaries, the con-

BRONZE INCENSE BURNER
12th century

112

tainers for the holy relics, were locked up in the treasuries of cathedrals and abbeys. When a church was a place of pilgrimage and housed the shrine of a saint, like the tomb of Saint Thomas à Becket at Canterbury, the treasury was thrown open on great days of pilgrimage. The pilgrims presented money and gifts and the reliquaries were displayed around the shrine for all to see.

MURDER OF
THOMAS À BECKET
from Queen Mary's Psalter

They were the masterpieces of goldsmiths and enamel workers. There were enameled boxes, large and small, round, square and oblong; reliquaries shaped like hands, feet or arms; and full-length figures of polished silver gilt, sparkling with gems.

Among the loveliest of these reliquary figures is one of Saint Stephen, the first Christian martyr. As a deacon of the early Church, Saint Stephen is shown wearing a dalmatic, the loose vestment of a deacon, with a border of jewels and filigree. Stephen was stoned to death for his faith, and on the back of the

113

ANGEL WITH A CENSER
from a Mosan reliquary, 13th century

RELIQUARY FIGURE
OF SAINT STEPHEN
Mosan, 13th century

figure is an engraving of his martyrdom and of the vision of Christ in heaven that Stephen saw before he died. The slender hands of the statue probably held a jeweled casket in the shape of a book containing a relic of the saint.

At the shrine of Saint Thomas à Becket in Canterbury Cathedral the pilgrims must have seen reliquaries as beautiful as this one, but the tomb of the saint, the goal of their journey, was even more splendid. It was entirely covered with plates of pure gold, engraved in a hundred patterns and studded all over with precious jewels—sapphires, diamonds, rubies and emeralds—and carved cameos of agate, jasper and cornelian. In the flaming light of many candles the shrine must have seemed to the kneeling pilgrims like a vision of Paradise.

RELIQUARY
French, 13th century

115

ENAMELED PYX
French, 13th century

Rich and poor made the journey to Canterbury to kneel before the tomb of Saint Thomas à Becket. They came from the castle and the countryside, the town and the Church. Among the pilgrims whom Chaucer describes so vividly in his *Canterbury Tales* you will find a knight and a squire; a merchant; a ship's captain; a carpenter and a weaver; a farmer, a miller and an Oxford scholar; a prioress, head of a convent; a nun, a monk and a friar, and many more.

All of them were people whom Chaucer must have seen and met and talked with. They belonged to his own time, the fourteenth century, but they would not have felt out of place a century earlier or later. Changes came slowly in the Middle Ages. In the years between 1000 and 1500 life for everyone was short and hard, a constant battle against dirt and disease and the sufferings caused by war. It was no wonder that people longed for beauty and color, for rich carvings, brilliant paintings and tapestries of a thousand flowers.

The craftsmen who labored to make these things
are nearly all nameless and forgotten now, but their
work lives on. In this book we have looked at only
a few of the things they made. There are many more
to be seen in museums. These medieval treasures
have passed through many hands; they may be bat-
tered and worn and broken, yet most of them can
still tell us something about the people who made
and used them. These were people like the pilgrims
in Chaucer's book, not so different from ourselves,
in spite of clothes and customs that may seem strange.
If you think of these medieval people when you look
at the things that belonged to them, you will begin
to see the tapestries, the carvings, the books and all
the rest in a new way, not as separate objects en-
shrined in museums, but as part of the living world
of the Middle Ages, the Age of Faith, the Age of
Chivalry and the Age of Craftsmen.

THE CANTERBURY
PILGRIMS

117

LIST OF SOURCES

THE BODLEIAN LIBRARY, OXFORD
Illustrations on Pages 24 (bottom of page), 43 (right and bottom left), 44 (top left), 45 (bottom left)

THE BRITISH MUSEUM, LONDON
Illustrations on Pages 10, 11, 21 (top), 37 (top right), 39 (bottom left), 41, 42, 43 (top and bottom right), 44 (bottom left), 52 (top), 55 (top right), 58 (top), 62 (top left and bottom), 63 (top and bottom), 64, 65, 66, 67, 76, 78, 87 (bottom right), 113 (top)

THE METROPOLITAN MUSEUM OF ART, NEW YORK
Illustrations on Pages 2 (frontispiece), 18, 20 (top left and lower left), 21 (right), 22, 23 (right and top left), 24 (top and lower left), 25, 26, 27, 28 (bottom), 34 (lower left), 35 (right), 36 (top), 39 (lower right), 40, 44 (top right), 45 (top left and right and bottom right), 46, 48, 49, 50, 51, 52 (lower left), 53, 54 (top), 56 (top), 57, 59 (lower right), 60, 61, 63 (right), 68 (top), 72, 73, 74 (bottom), 75, 80, 83, 85, 86, 87 (top), 88 (lower left), 90 (top left), 92, 93 (lower right), 94 (top left), 95, 96, 97, 99, 100, 103, 104, 106, 107, 108, 109, 110, 111, 112, 113 (lower right), 114, 115

THE PIERPONT MORGAN LIBRARY, NEW YORK
Illustrations on Pages 68 (lower left), 69, 70, 71 (top), 91

THE VICTORIA AND ALBERT MUSEUM, LONDON
Illustrations on Pages 30 (top), 33 (bottom), 37 (lower right), 38, 39 (upper and center right), 62 (left and top right), 74 (top), 88 (top), 89, 93 (top), 94 (bottom), 101, 102, 105

THE YALE UNIVERSITY ART GALLERY, NEW HAVEN
Illustrations on Pages 29 (bottom), 55 (bottom), 82

ABOUT THE AUTHOR—ILLUSTRATOR:

CHRISTINE PRICE WAS BORN IN LONDON AND RECEIVED her early education in England. As a child she spent much time exploring the English countryside and accompanying her mother on visits to medieval castles and ancient village churches. Her mother was making a study of the art and architecture of the Middle Ages, and Christine's great interest in that period began at an early age. Coming to the United States, she continued her education at Vassar College and at the Art Students League of New York. She later returned to London to study at the Central School of Arts and Crafts. During her holidays from school, Miss Price traveled in Europe and the British Isles and in recent years she has visited such different parts of the United States as Maine, Florida and Wyoming. She is the author of DAVID AND THE MOUNTAIN and other books, and the illustrator of many books for young readers, among them THE STORY OF PETER TSCHAIKOWSKY, THE BIRD WATCHERS and GREENWOOD SUMMER.

She now lives in Castleton, Vermont.

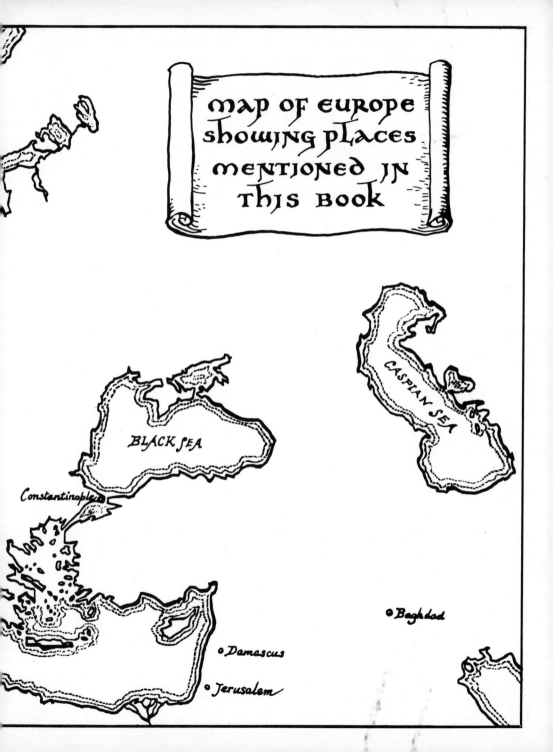

MAP OF EUROPE SHOWING PLACES MENTIONED IN THIS BOOK

CASPIAN SEA

BLACK SEA

Constantinople

Baghdad

Damascus

Jerusalem